Praise for the Believe Series

"As grandparents of 50 grandchildren, we heartily endorse the *Believe and You're There* series. Parents and grandparents, gather your children around you and discover the scriptures again as they come alive in the *Believe and You're There* series."

> —STEPHEN AND SANDRA COVEY
> Stephen Covey is the bestselling author of *7 Habits of Highly Effective People*.

"Bravo! This series is a treasure! You pray that your children will fall in love with and get lost in the scriptures just as they are discovering the wonder of reading. This series does it. Two thumbs way, way up!"

> —MACK AND REBECCA WILBERG
> Mack Wilberg is the Music Director of the Mormon Tabernacle Choir.

"This series is a powerful tool for helping children learn to liken the scriptures to themselves. Helping children experience the scriptural stories from their point of view is genius."

> —ED AND PATRICIA PINEGAR
> Ed Pinegar is the bestselling author of *Raising the Bar*.

"We only wish these wonderful books had been available when we were raising our own children. How we look forward to sharing them with all our grandchildren!"

> —STEPHEN AND JANET ROBINSON
> Stephen Robinson is the bestselling author of *Believing Christ*.

"The *Believe and You're There* series taps into the popular genre of fantasy and imagination in a wonderful way. Today's children will be drawn into the reality of events described in the scriptures. Ever true to the scriptural accounts, the authors have crafted delightful stories that will surely awaken children's vivid imaginations while teaching truths that will often sound familiar."

—TRUMAN AND ANN MADSEN
Truman Madsen was the bestselling author of *Joseph Smith, the Prophet.*

"My dad and I read *At the Miracles of Jesus* together. First I'd read a chapter, and then he would. Now we're reading the next book. He says he feels the Spirit when we read. So do I."

—CASEY J., AGE 9

"My mom likes me to read before bed. I used to hate it, but the *Believe* books make reading fun and exciting. And they make you feel good inside, too."

—KADEN T., AGE 10

"Reading the *Believe* series with my tweens and my teens has been a big spiritual boost in our home—even for me! It always leaves me peaceful and more certain about what I believe."

—GLADYS A., AGE 43

"I love how Katie, Matthew, and Peter are connected to each other and to their grandma. These stories link children to their families, their ancestors, and on to the Savior. I heartily recommend them for any child, parent, or grandparent."

—ANNE S., AGE 50
Mother of ten, grandmother of nine (and counting)

When the Prince of Peace Was Born

Believe and You're There

When the Prince of Peace Was Born

Book 4

ALICE W. JOHNSON & ALLISON H. WARNER

DESERET
BOOK

SALT LAKE CITY, UTAH

Text © 2009 Alice W. Johnson, Allison H. Warner

Illustrations © 2009 Jerry Harston

Visit us at DeseretBook.com

Library of Congress Cataloging-in-Publication Data

Johnson, Alice W.

  Believe and you're there when the Prince of Peace was born / Alice W. Johnson and Allison H. Warner ; [illustrations by Jerry Harston].

     p. cm.

  Summary: Katie, Matthew, and Peter visit their grandmother for Christmas and travel through her magical painting to Bethlehem where they experience the events of Christ's birth, including the announcement of the angels to the shepherds.

  ISBN 978-1-60641-200-8 (paperbound)

  1. Jesus Christ—Nativity—Juvenile literature. I. Warner, Allison H.

  II. Harston, Jerry, ill. III. Title.

  BT315.3.J63 2009

  232.92—dc22

                                                                    2009026232

Printed in the United States of America

Worzalla Publishing Co., Stevens Point, WI

10   9   8   7   6   5   4   3   2   1

Believe in the wonder,
Believe if you dare,
Believe in your heart,
Just believe . . . and you're there!

Contents

CHAPTER ONE

A Christmas Carol 1

CHAPTER TWO

Seasoned Travelers 8

CHAPTER THREE

The Road to Bethlehem 14

CHAPTER FOUR

A Good Shepherd 22

CHAPTER FIVE

No Room at the Inn 28

CHAPTER SIX

Scared Speechless 34

CHAPTER SEVEN

A Shepherd Family 41

CHAPTER EIGHT

    The Heavens Open 50

CHAPTER NINE

    Back to Bethlehem 57

CHAPTER TEN

    And They Found the Babe 62

CHAPTER ELEVEN

    The Gift of Love 70

Chapter One

A Christmas Carol

"I have no idea what to get Grandma for Christmas," Katie sighed as she and her brothers, Matthew and Peter, stood huddled on the sidewalk in front of Grandma's house.

"Why don't we give her some perfume?" Matthew suggested.

"Grandmas always wear too much perfume, if you ask me," Peter declared, holding his nose.

"Christmas isn't for a week. Can we go inside first and decide later? I'm freezing out here!"

Matthew complained, blowing on his hands to keep them warm.

Falling snow shimmered in the glow of the Christmas lights that adorned every home on Grandma's street. Through the large picture window, the children could see Grandma rocking contentedly in her chair next to the Christmas tree. Encouraged by the warmth of the festive scene, they hurried up the path to the front door.

"Hey, Peter," Katie called out to her brother, who had arrived at the doorstep first. "You know how Grandma loves hearing carols. Let's surprise her with some, shall we? We can start with her favorite, 'Away in a Manger.'"

"Perfect!" Matthew agreed. "Then let's sing 'Far, Far Away on Judea's Plains.' She loves that one too."

Eight-year-old Peter chimed in, "As long as we finish with 'We Wish You a Merry Christmas,' it all sounds good to me."

"How about one verse of each?" Matthew

added, longing for the warmth of Grandma's house.

"Good idea, and everybody keep thinking of a perfect gift for Grandma," Katie reminded her brothers.

"Right, sis," Matthew assured her. "I'll put on my thinking cap!"

Katie gave a starting pitch, Peter rang the doorbell, and the children sang out in their clear, true voices:

Away in a manger, no crib for a bed,
The little Lord Jesus lay down his sweet head . . .

Grandma threw open the door and gazed at her grandchildren with delight as they started singing the next carol:

Far, far away on Judea's plains
Shepherds of old heard the joyous strains . . .

Grandma clapped her hands together, beaming with pleasure.

And then, finishing off the performance in style, Katie, Matthew, and Peter belted out a rousing chorus of "We Wish You a Merry Christmas."

Grandma applauded enthusiastically and ushered in each grandchild with a prolonged embrace.

"I knew this would be a special evening," Grandma gushed, "but you've started it more

perfectly than I could have imagined. Why, by the carols you've chosen, I'd think you had already seen my new painting."

"A new painting?" Peter couldn't hold back his excitement. "I can't wait to see it, Grandma! Can we go to the art cottage right now?"

"Oh, how I love your enthusiasm, Peter!" Grandma chuckled. "But first things first, okay?" she said. "Where are your journals?"

"Three journals on board!" Matthew assured Grandma, patting the backpack slung over his shoulder.

"Then I'll just get my Bible," Grandma said, picking up the beautiful worn book from its customary spot on

the living room table. And away they all went, through Grandma's kitchen, out the back door, and into the crisp, white evening, alight with newly fallen snow.

Across the lawn, past the garden, and through the pine trees they marched, until they reached the arched blue door of Grandma's quaint little white art cottage. Soft firelight flickering in the windows beckoned Grandma and the children. But they paused at the door, despite the cold.

"I know we want to go in and get warm, but we mustn't forget our password," Katie reminded them. "Who wants to start?"

Irrepressible Peter dove right in. "Believe in the wonder!" he almost shouted, his breath curling above him in the cold night air.

Matthew picked it right up, matching Peter's volume. "Believe if you dare!"

"Believe in your heart!" Even Katie was more boisterous than usual.

Grandma joined in as they all finished the chant with extra vigor, "Just believe . . . and you're there!"

Chapter Two

Seasoned Travelers

Inside the warm cottage, the children wasted no time settling themselves on the pillows Grandma had arranged. "What are we reading about tonight?" Matthew asked as he planted himself in front of the veiled easel.

"Well," Grandma answered with a touch of mystery in her voice, "why do you suppose I was so pleased with the carols you chose to sing tonight?"

"Ah," Katie was thinking out loud. "The first one was 'Away in a Manger.' Maybe we're going to hear about the Savior's birth."

"Right," Matthew picked up her thought. "And then we sang about the shepherds who were on the plains of Judea when He was born."

"I've got it!" Peter exclaimed. "We're going to Bethlehem!"

Katie and Matthew gasped. They weren't sure if Grandma knew about their travels, and they didn't want to know what might happen if she found out.

"Oh, Grandma," Katie spoke quickly to cover Peter's blunder. "Your paintings are so wonderful that Peter feels like he's actually a part of the story. Isn't that right, Peter?"

Peter nodded convincingly. Grandma smiled, grateful for the compliment. "Well, Peter," she suggested, "if you're so crazy about my paintings, why don't you be the one to uncover this one?"

Without a moment's pause, Peter jumped up and yanked off the blanket. The dramatic unveiling revealed a painting of a dirt road winding through gentle brown hills. Small groups of people with donkeys and camels were making their way along the road, all going the same direction.

"That sure looks like ancient Palestine," Matthew observed.

"You are exactly right," said Grandma. "You say that like a seasoned traveler, my boy."

Grandma spoke in jest, but Katie and Matthew looked at each other meaningfully, both with the same thought: *We've been there three times and counting. How much does Grandma really know?*

But before they could wonder anymore about Grandma's comment, Peter asked a question that drew everyone's attention back to the painting. "What's at the end of that road?"

"It's a little city," said Katie. "I think it could be Bethlehem."

"I told you so!" said Peter, feeling vindicated. "That's where Jesus was born."

"So that's where Mary and Joseph lived?" asked Matthew.

"No," Katie shook her head. "They lived in a place called Nazareth."

"Then why was Jesus born in Bethlehem?" Matthew wondered.

"Good question, Matthew," said Grandma as she took her place in her overstuffed rocking chair. "I'll start reading the story, and I think you'll discover the answer to Matthew's question. Now, make yourselves comfortable, and imagine that you're there." And with that, Grandma picked up her scriptures and began.

"'And it came to pass in those days, that there went out a decree from Caesar Augustus, that all the world should be taxed. . . . And all went to be taxed, every one into his own city. And Joseph also went up from Galilee . . . to be taxed with Mary, his espoused wife.'"

As Grandma read, six young eyes were riveted to the images on the easel, hoping to see some movement. That, the children had learned, was their invitation to enter the painting. Suddenly, as if on cue, the travelers along the road started to move their arms and legs. Enchanted by the thought of the adventure awaiting them, all three children rose in unison to get a closer look.

Katie, who usually thought things through

carefully, felt strangely impetuous. And without pausing, she thrust her hand into the painting.

Thankfully, Matthew was paying attention, and, without a moment to spare, he grabbed Katie's free hand, and with his other hand reached out for Peter. Katie was quickly disappearing into the painting, and with their hands linked together, first Katie, then Matthew, and finally Peter, were pulled right into the landscape of Grandma's painting!

Chapter Three

The Road to Bethlehem

"Yippee!" hollered Katie, still feeling reckless and free. The children felt and heard the rush of wind around them, and Peter cried, "Hey, we're headed right for the road in the picture!"

"Let's just hope we don't land on one of the donkeys we saw," said Katie, regaining her practicality.

Katie had no sooner finished speaking than the three children felt the ground under their feet. Around them were several shrubs and tall palm trees. Grandma and her cottage were nowhere to be seen.

Looking down at his strange attire, Matthew

observed, "I think these are the very same clothes we were wearing when we visited the garden tomb. And this robe is still itchy!"

Katie and Peter looked down at their own robes, which were made from thick, rough, gray and brown cloth. "Well," said Katie, completely back to her old self, "let's just be thankful we look like everyone else here, and that we don't have to dress like this every day."

"Hey!" exclaimed Peter, wiping his brow. "I'm sweating! What's going on? A few minutes ago I was freezing, and now I'm almost hot! It sure doesn't feel like December anymore."

"That's because it *isn't* December," Katie instructed her younger brother.

"Not December? Matthew, could that be right?" Clearly, Peter thought Katie must be confused.

"I don't know exactly when Jesus was born, but it wasn't in the winter, for sure," Matthew told his brother.

"Then why do we celebrate Christmas in December? Isn't the point of Christmas to remember

15

the Savior's birth?" Peter asked, sounding hopelessly perplexed.

"Definitely," Matthew agreed. "I think people just got in the habit of celebrating Christmas at the end of the year. Is that right, Katie?"

"I guess so," Katie spoke off-handedly. She was clearly not interested in the boys' questions. "Let's not worry about that right now, okay? We really need to figure out where we are." So shoulder to shoulder, the children cautiously crept to the edge of the trees and peered out.

Close by was a well where many travelers were gathered. Some were drawing water, filling bags of animal skins to take with them on their journeys. Others sat on the ground, resting in the shade or eating their afternoon meals. Around them, their donkeys and camels waited, tethered to the tall trees.

Peter, who loved all animals, challenged Matthew, "I'll race you to the donkeys!" And in a flash, both boys were running headlong toward the well.

"Not so fast," called Katie, hurrying to join them.

At the well, Katie breathlessly reminded her little brothers, "Settle down, boys. Remember, we've got to fit in."

"Good point, Katie," Matthew agreed. "Peter, let's just sit here a while and see what's going on." The brothers sat down quietly near the other travelers. As Katie joined them, a young man leading a donkey approached the well. A pregnant woman rode on the donkey's back.

"Matthew, do you know who I think that is?" Katie asked her brother. "I think that is Mary and Joseph."

Matthew nodded, peering at the traveling man and woman. The kind-looking man brought the donkey to a stop and secured its lead on a nearby tree. Then he went to the donkey's side and gently lifted his companion to the ground.

"Isn't Mary beautiful?" Peter said to the amazement of his brother and sister. "And look! She is going to have a baby."

As Mary stood and stretched, Joseph took a blanket from the back of the donkey and carefully spread it on the ground. Taking her hand, Joseph gently lowered her to the blanket to rest.

"I'll bet she is glad to get off that donkey for a while," Matthew whispered to Katie.

"That's for sure," she whispered back.

Joseph went to the well, drew some water, poured it in a cup, and offered it to Mary. Then, dipping a small cloth in the cool water, he wiped her forehead and face with care.

"Thank you, Joseph," she said gratefully, smiling up at him and tenderly touching his hand.

"Are you sure you are all right, Mary?" asked Joseph, his voice filled with compassion.

She smiled again. "Yes. I am just tired. Let us rest here for a moment, and then I should be ready to travel the rest of the way to Bethlehem."

"I shall get some water for the donkey," Joseph said, heading to the well again.

While Joseph was gone, the children watched Mary. She looked to be just a few years older than Katie. "She is a very special person, isn't she?" Katie

observed, her voice choked with emotion. "You can tell from her face that she is peaceful inside, even though her body must be uncomfortable." Here was Mary, thought Katie, very close to child-birth, riding a bumpy and uncomfortable donkey, without any kind of saddle, along a dusty dirt road—and yet her tired eyes still shone with deep, unmistakable happiness.

Joseph, having fed and watered the donkey, returned. "Have you rested enough, Mary?" he asked with concern. "I think we can be there within the hour."

"Yes, Joseph. I am ready," she said.

"Then let us continue our journey. I hope we can find a place to stay before dark." He gathered up the blankets and lifted Mary onto the donkey.

"Come on," said Katie to her brothers. "Let's follow them. I think Jesus is going to be born soon."

"Right now?" asked Peter excitedly.

"Goodness, no!" said Katie, feeling a little exas-perated. "Haven't you heard the story enough to know how it goes? He won't be born until they get to Bethlehem, and that's right where they're headed."

"I remember the story," said Matthew. "But do you really think that nobody will let them in? She's going to have a baby, after all!"

"It's hard to imagine, isn't it?" Katie replied. "Come on, let's go too."

"We'd better let them get far enough down the road that they don't notice us," Matthew told Katie, as he leaned on the tall walking stick he had scavenged from the sturdy bushes behind them.

When they were finally satisfied that they could safely travel behind without being discovered, Matthew, Katie, and Peter started down the road. Walking slowly in their heavy robes, they quietly melted into the throng of travelers making their way toward the little town of Bethlehem.

Chapter Four

A Good Shepherd

Sloping, rocky hillsides lined the winding road leading to Bethlehem. Intrigued by the unfamiliar landscape, the children examined every detail of their unusual surroundings.

"Hey, look over there! It's a herd of sheep," Peter said, pointing to a nearby hill.

"It's called a *flock* of sheep, not a herd," Matthew corrected his brother, an amused smile on his face.

"And there's a shepherd boy," exclaimed Katie. "Goodness, he's about my age!"

The shepherd was smiling patiently at two small lambs that had wandered from the rest of the flock. The little ones were bleating loudly, as though they were frightened. The shepherd boy cupped his hand around his mouth and called out, "Sarai! Little Sarai!" One of the lambs turned, saw the shepherd, and quickly scrambled across the hill toward the rest of the flock.

Then the shepherd called out, "Efram! Efram! Over here!" The other lamb, hearing his name, also turned and hurried to the shepherd's side.

"How sweet," cooed Katie. "The baby lambs have their own names."

"Do you think every one of the sheep has a different name?" Matthew wondered aloud.

Peter ran toward the shepherd. "I don't know," he called to his brother over his shoulder, "but I'm going to find out!"

"Wait!" called Matthew and Katie. Peter, quite simply, did not have a shy bone in his body—or a cautious one. He scrambled up the hill, bouncing over and around the plentiful rocks and small shrubs.

"Hi!" said Peter as he neared the shepherd boy. "My name is Peter. What's yours?"

"I am Eli," the shepherd boy answered with a friendly grin.

"Hello, Eli. You sure have a lot of sheep," Peter said, surveying the flock. "I noticed that you called two of the lambs by name. Does each of your sheep have its very own name?"

"Oh, yes," replied Eli. "Every single one. A lamb would not come when I called if I didn't use its own special name."

"But there are so many of them! Isn't it hard to remember which one is which?" Peter wondered, sure that he would never be able to remember so many names.

"Oh, it may look hard, but I got to know each lamb when it was just a baby," explained Eli as he guided a lamb back to its mother. "I helped each one grow up safe and warm and healthy. To me, each lamb is different, and each one is very special.

"You see this one right here?" Eli continued, pointing to a lamb following behind him. "His name is Shem. Shem is always obedient and stays right near me. But see that little one running all over the hill?" He pointed to a frisky lamb bounding across the hillside. "That is Marcus. He wanders a lot, but when I call his name, he knows my voice and comes back to the fold."

As he spoke, Eli caressed the tiny lamb he carried in his arms.

Reaching out to pet the lamb, Peter asked, "Why are you carrying this one? Is he hurt?"

"Oh, no, he is not hurt," Eli assured Peter. "He

doesn't recognize his name yet, and he cannot tell my voice from the voices of other shepherds on this hillside. I keep him close to me so he will learn that I am his shepherd. He must understand that I love him and that I want to protect him. And then when I call, he will come."

They heard another lamb bleating in the distance. "I must go, Peter," Eli said, his eyes searching the hillside for the wandering lamb. "You're headed to Bethlehem, aren't you? Perhaps I will see you there later!" With that, Eli hurried away to find his crying animal. Peter watched him go, and then bounded down the hill to join Katie and Matthew on the road to the city.

"I made a new friend!" Peter announced breathlessly. "His name is Eli, and he told me all about his sheep!"

"That's great, Peter," said Matthew, patting him on the back.

Then Katie cried out, "Hey, everybody! Look up ahead! We're almost to Bethlehem!" Excited by the prospect of seeing the fabled town, the children quickened their pace.

Just ahead of them, Mary and Joseph were still slowly making their way along the rough and rutted road. Every few minutes, Mary's head would droop, and Joseph would comfort her with kind words and a cool drink from the goatskin bag slung over his shoulder. "Our journey is almost finished," he reassured her. "We will find a place to stay soon."

"I pray it will be so," Mary sighed.

Hearing this, Katie's heart grew heavy. "Even though we already know how this story ends, I still can't help worrying for Mary and Joseph," she told her brothers. "Jesus is going to be born soon, and I hope Mary can rest first." As she trudged along the dusty road to Bethlehem, Katie silently offered a prayer for dear Mary and for the precious child about to come into the world.

Chapter Five

No Room at the Inn

As they rounded a bend in the road, the children were met by a wave of unfamiliar sounds. Hundreds of people crowded into the small streets and outdoor marketplaces, and the braying of donkeys and stomping of camels made things even louder. At last they were in Bethlehem!

Peter put his hands over his ears and shouted to the other children, "This place is noisy!"

"It sure is," agreed Matthew.

Katie shook her head at the boys and said, "Let's not worry about the noise. Let's worry about poor Mary and Joseph! They are right over there."

The children looked ahead to see Joseph standing at the door of a house that was overflowing with dozens of people. They crowded the yard, leaned from the open windows, and even sat on the covered roof.

Katie, Matthew, and Peter could barely hear Joseph ask if there was room at the busy inn. But they could see the man at the door shaking his head and shrugging his shoulders. It seemed Bethlehem was simply bursting with the many people who, like Joseph and Mary, had come from far away to the city of their birth to be taxed. The children followed Joseph, watching as he stopped at several more inns, searching for a place to stay. And each time, the answer was the same: "No! No more room here!"

Feeling troubled, Matthew asked Katie, "Why won't people let Mary and Joseph in? Don't they know that Jesus is going to be born?"

"No, they don't, Matthew," explained Katie patiently. "The innkeepers don't know how special

Mary and Joseph are, and they don't understand that the new baby will be the Savior of the world."

"*I* would let them in!" declared Peter.

"Of course you would, little buddy," said Katie, patting Peter's curly head. "Hey, I have an idea!" she said. "Why don't we check some places too?

Maybe we'll find a place with room for Mary to rest."

"Good idea, sis," Matthew said. "Let's try over there."

The children carefully walked around animals and carts toward a small gray building that appeared to be an inn, with donkeys tethered near the front door, and a steady stream of travelers going in and out. In a corner of the front courtyard,

several Roman guards were gathered, talking and laughing as they watched the activity at the inn.

An angry-looking woman sat on a stool near the open door to the inn. Before the children could even ask, she shook her head vigorously and snapped, "I hope you aren't looking for a room. There's not a place to be had in all Bethlehem."

"Are you certain?" Katie asked haltingly.

"Oh, I'm certain, all right," replied the woman with a sharp laugh. "The Romans told everyone to go to the city of their birth to be counted and taxed. Where did they think all these travelers would stay? You'd best make a bed for yourselves near your animals. This city is just plain full! Now be off with you, children!"

If she had been looking for a place to stay just for herself, Katie would have obeyed the ill-tempered woman's command. But the thought of Mary without a place to rest fortified Katie's resolve and she turned back to the woman and bravely stood her ground. "Well," she said, taking a big breath, "it wouldn't hurt to look, would it?"

Surprised by Katie's boldness, the woman slowly looked Katie up and down, pursed her lips, and shook her head. "Oh, all right," she answered with a huff, "if you must. Go ahead and look for yourselves. You will see that I am right." Then muttering under her breath, she complained to no one in particular, "Children these days! They think they know everything!"

Chapter Six

Scared Speechless

"Okay, boys, follow me," said Katie, as she led the way through the inn's crowded courtyard, her brothers following close behind.

"I hate to admit it, sis," Matthew said, surveying the courtyard, "but I think that woman was right. I can't see a single place to squeeze in a bed. And I'm sure the rooms inside are even more crowded than the yard."

"You're probably right," Katie sighed, "but I've still got to try." And she continued walking around the bedrolls and the sacks of food that had been carefully placed by travelers to mark the sleeping spots they had claimed. Katie was looking for any spots left open where Mary might rest.

Suddenly, from the other side of the courtyard, a tall, stern-faced Roman soldier spotted the three children picking their way through the maze of belongings. "You there! Halt!" he shouted, and he strode swiftly to where they stood. Stopping directly in front of them, he planted the bottom of his spear hard on the ground, just inches from Matthew's foot.

The three children froze with fear, and Katie found herself praying that the soldier wouldn't hear her heart pounding through her chest.

"What are you children doing here? Are you looking for food to steal? I think you're nothing more than common thieves, just looking around for what you will take next!" the soldier shouted his angry accusation. "Now, answer my question! What are you doing here?"

Matthew opened his mouth to speak, but no words would come out. Katie, too, moved her lips, but couldn't make a sound.

"What do you children want here?" the soldier repeated his demand.

Peter saved the day. Finally finding his voice, he stammered, "We . . . we were looking for a . . . a place to stay."

The soldier was skeptical. "Where are your parents?" he challenged, his eyes peering down at Peter from under his helmet.

Peter wasn't sure what to tell him, so he simply replied, "They're not here right now."

"Well, you shouldn't be wandering around the city alone," the soldier said to Peter. Then he turned, calling over his shoulder to his fellow soldiers and laughing scornfully, "These Jews! Can't they keep track of their own children?" The other soldiers laughed right along with him, but the Jews in the courtyard stood stone-faced, not wanting to provoke the Roman soldier any further.

Matthew's mind began to race. *This could be real trouble,* he thought. *How would we explain exactly where our parents are?* He turned to Katie. "Let's get out of here . . . and quick!" he murmured out of the corner of his mouth.

"Over here," a man called out, smiling sympathetically. He beckoned to the children and motioned to a side entrance in the courtyard wall.

The soldiers were laughing so hard at their mockery of Jewish people, they didn't even notice as Katie, Matthew, and Peter quietly ducked through the door and into the street beyond.

"Run as fast as you can," Matthew hollered as he ran toward the main village street.

"Don't worry! We're right behind you," Peter called out, dragging Katie with him. Once back in the village center, the children blended into the crowds and walked along unnoticed, finally able to catch their breath.

"Well, that didn't help. I guess Mary and Joseph will just have to rely on the Lord to find a place to rest," Katie sighed.

"Don't worry, Katie," Matthew comforted his sister, slipping his arm around her shoulder. "You know He will. Hey! Look up ahead!"

Sure enough, near the end of the winding, narrow street, they saw Joseph as he was turned away from yet another inn with no room. Mary sat nearby on the donkey, waiting quietly. Slowly, Joseph walked to the very last door on the street. The door opened, and Joseph asked, "Sir, do you have some room where my wife and I could rest from our journey? We have traveled for many long days—all the way from Nazareth. She is very tired, and as you can see, she will soon have a baby."

"I don't have a bit of space left," said the innkeeper. "I am truly sorry."

Joseph lowered his head. "Please, we are willing to take the humblest of rooms."

Matthew glanced at Katie, who looked as though she might cry.

"What are they going to do?" she whispered.

"Don't worry, sis," Matthew said to his sister. "We already know that they'll find a stable."

"I know," replied Katie, "but I never imagined how hard it really was for them."

Suddenly, Matthew pointed excitedly. "Look, Katie!" The innkeeper was motioning for Mary and Joseph to go around to the back of the inn.

"Thank you, sir, thank you," they heard Joseph saying. "May you be blessed for your kindness."

Joseph led the donkey, with Mary still on its back, down a path along the side of the inn. There, across a dusty courtyard, was a small stable carved out of the hillside, almost like a cave. The innkeeper led them past the stalls in which animals were feeding to a secluded area in the far corner of the stable. "There is some clean straw over there. You can use all you like," the innkeeper offered, his voice full of compassion.

"Thank you," Joseph replied gratefully. "Could you tell me where I might draw water?"

"The well is in the courtyard," the innkeeper said, pointing around the corner of the house. "God bless you both." With that, he returned to the house, leaving Joseph and Mary alone.

With relief on her face, Katie motioned for the boys to quietly follow her. "Mary should rest," she explained. "The baby will be here soon." The three young children tiptoed across the courtyard, past the well, and into the busy streets of Bethlehem.

Chapter Seven

A Shepherd Family

Back in the crowded street, the children began to explore the busy outdoor marketplace. Jammed between Bethlehem's low buildings were stalls that lined the street where merchants displayed baskets overflowing with cheese, fish, nuts, and round loaves of flat bread. In another section of the marketplace, wool blankets, clay pots, and small oil lamps hung in attractive displays. Huddled around the stalls, people were noisily buying and selling. It almost sounded as if they were mad at each other.

"That's just too much money," a man hollered at a woman who was selling colorful scarves. "Give me two for that price, or I'll buy my scarves from someone else!"

Another man waved his arms and barked, "I'll give you ten shekels, but not one shekel more!"

For a moment, Matthew feared there were so many people jammed in the marketplace that he and his siblings wouldn't be able to move through its narrow, twisting walkways. Thankfully, Katie linked elbows with him on one side and with Peter on the other so they wouldn't get separated. Side by side, the three children made their way down the teeming lane, observing the unfamiliar customs of ancient Bethlehem all around them.

At the edge of the market, Peter spotted his shepherd friend, Eli, buying a fresh loaf of round, flat bread. "Eli! Eli!" shouted Peter, running to greet him. "I'm glad I found you again. Come meet my brother and my sister."

Eli tucked the bread under his arm and hurried over to the children. "Eli, this is my brother, Matthew, and my big sister, Katie," said Peter. "Everyone, this is Eli. He's the shepherd I met on our way to the city."

"Hello," said Eli. "I am very glad to meet all of you. My mother sent me to buy bread for our family dinner. Would you like to meet my family?"

"Oh, yes," exclaimed Peter. "We would love to!"

"Are they far from here?" inquired Katie, not wanting to go too far from Bethlehem.

"Not far at all," replied Eli. "We're tending our flocks on that hill tonight." Eli pointed to a nearby rise where an open tent was perched. All around the tent, sheep were grazing contentedly, and the flames of an inviting fire danced gaily, shining through the gathering dusk of evening.

"We live several miles away," Eli told Katie, "but my father is going to sell some of his sheep at the market tomorrow so people can offer them as sacrifices at the temple."

"Why do they offer the lambs as sacrifices?" Matthew asked Eli.

"It is to remind us that one day, the promised Messiah will come and offer Himself as a sacrifice for us," Eli answered solemnly.

"Do you offer all your sheep as sacrifices?" Peter asked, clearly dismayed at the thought.

"Oh, no, we only offer the firstlings of the flock and the lambs without blemish. That is why it is so important that we take good care of them," he explained to Peter.

"Doesn't it make you sad to sacrifice lambs that you know so well?" Katie asked Eli.

"Yes, in a way, I suppose it does. But it also helps me remember that the Messiah is coming to save us—and that makes me happy. Come along, then, and meet my family," Eli said.

Following Eli, the children left the streets of Bethlehem behind and started up the gentle hillside. In the western sky, the sun was setting, bathing Bethlehem in its golden glow and making the world feel safe and peaceful. The noisy city markets of Bethlehem and the harrowing encounter with the Roman soldier were soon forgotten as the children were filled with the beauty of the simple scene before them.

Nearing the tent, they saw a mother and father tending a small fire, while a little girl with dark, curly hair and rosy cheeks sat nearby, holding a tiny black lamb in her lap. Seeing the children coming, the father called out, "Eli, son! You have returned. And you have brought visitors, I see."

"Yes, father," Eli replied. "This is Katie, Matthew, and Peter. I met Peter this afternoon on the road into Bethlehem."

"Ah, then you're visiting Bethlehem like so many others," Eli's father said kindly to the three children. "My name is Nathaniel. This is my wife, Anna, and our youngest child, Rebecca. We welcome you to our tent."

Katie smiled at little Rebecca, who looked up shyly at first. But after a moment, Rebecca was smiling too, and she reached for Katie's hand, pulling her down to sit next to her on the thick, brown blanket.

"Please, come and share our evening meal with us," Anna invited them warmly. "We have little to eat, but what we have is yours."

As the happy group sat cross-legged around the fire, Nathaniel broke the large, flat loaf of bread that Eli had purchased at the market into pieces.

He gave a fresh, crusty piece to Anna and each of the children. This was followed by a chunk of delicious cheese. Nathaniel also passed around a cup filled with cool water so everyone could drink a little. Finally, the family shared a bowl of moist, soft figs, which burst with sweet juices in the children's mouths. Although the food was simple, Matthew ate eagerly and with great pleasure.

"You are hungry, boy," said Nathaniel with a smile. "You must have traveled far today. Here, please have more."

Katie's heart swelled with gratitude. These strangers were so loving and generous! She thought of all the comforts she enjoyed at home—like her soft bed with its fluffy, warm quilt, and the refrigerator that was always full of good things to eat. This shepherd family had so little, yet they welcomed Katie and her brothers as though they were treasured friends!

"Do you have a place to stay the night?" inquired Nathaniel. "If not, you are surely welcome here. Would you like to stay?"

"Thank you," Katie replied gratefully. "We would love to stay with you." Matthew and Peter nodded in agreement. They all felt very comfortable and secure in the tent of this good family.

"Eli will take the first watch tonight with the sheep," announced Nathaniel. "Since he turned thirteen, I have trusted him to watch them without me. Would either of you boys like to watch with him?"

"I would," said Matthew eagerly, feeling very grown-up.

"And so would I," Peter hastily added, not wanting to miss anything. "It sounds kind of like a Scout campout."

"Like a what?" Eli asked curiously.

"Oh, boy," Matthew muttered under his breath to Katie. Then he smiled at Eli. "We'll have to tell you about that later, Eli. It would take too long to explain now, and besides it's getting dark! The sheep are waiting for us."

"Very well, then, I'll hear about . . . how do you say it? . . . Scout–outs? . . . some other time. Grab your walking sticks and let's go," Eli said, leading the way.

"Well, then," Nathaniel said, "that's settled. Katie, you can sleep here on these blankets with Rebecca."

Tired from the eventful day, Katie was happy to curl up near the warm fire. Rebecca lay near her, and after a few moments, she quietly slipped her small brown hand into Katie's fair one.

Katie squeezed the hand of the sweet little shepherd girl, tucked a heavy blanket around her small shoulders, and then gazed up at the star-filled sky. Her mind filled with questions: Was this the night when the new star would shine? How were Mary and Joseph? Had Mary rested comfortably after the journey? Were they warm enough in the snug stable?

And then . . . she was asleep.

Chapter Eight

The Heavens Open

Matthew, Eli, and Peter perched on a large rock overlooking the fields outside Bethlehem. In the distance, the lights from the low buildings of the city flickered and danced, and then, one by one, they faded away. Nearby, small fires dotted the hillside where other shepherds were tending their flocks.

"You must love being a shepherd at night when the rest of the world is sleeping," Matthew said, feeling peaceful inside.

"Yes," agreed Eli, "you can see why the night

watch has always been my favorite. Sometimes I write songs to sing to my sheep. And to help me stay awake."

"Could we hear one?" Peter asked hopefully.

"Of course," said Eli.

Matthew and Peter gazed up at the night sky as Eli began to sing in his boyish tenor voice:

Still is the night for a shepherd boy,
Still are the stars overhead,
Still are the fields where he tends to his sheep,
Still is his soft, grassy bed.
Still is the moon hanging low in the sky,
Still is the shepherd's soft prayer.
Hear how he pleads for the lambs 'round his feet.
See how they trust in his care.
Still, still, the shepherd keeps watch,
Waiting for morning to come.
Still, still, he cares for his lambs
Waiting for the sun.

"That was nice," said Matthew. "It was like a lullaby. I almost fell asleep!"

"You boys do look tired," Eli said, resting his hand on his shepherd's crook. "I'm used to staying awake at night. Go ahead and sleep if you like."

"No, I'm going to stay awake with you," said Matthew with determination.

"Me, too," said Peter.

But as the hour grew later, the boys rested their heads on their arms and leaned against the rock. And though they tried their best to keep their eyes open, it wasn't long before they had fallen into a sound sleep. Eli smiled to himself, remembering nights when he had drifted off to sleep, even when he was trying his best to stay awake.

It seemed no time had passed before they were awakened by Eli whispering anxiously. "Matthew, Peter! Wake up! Look, something unusual is happening. The sky is growing bright!" As Matthew and Peter rubbed their eyes sleepily, they heard other shepherds talking and moving about with excitement.

Even Katie had awakened, and she scrambled up the slope to join the boys. Behind her came

Nathaniel, gazing heavenward. Then, as they all stood wondering at the light, an angel appeared in the midst of it, standing above them in the air.

Never before had any of them seen such a sight. Trembling and shaking, the shepherds huddled together, clinging to each other in fear. Just at that moment, the angel proclaimed in a joyous voice, "Fear not: for, behold, I bring you good tidings of great joy, which shall be to all people. For unto you is born this day in the city of David a Savior, which is Christ the Lord."

"A Savior, born in the city of David! That's Bethlehem! It is just as was prophesied," Eli said, his voice filled with wonder.

The news seemed to calm the frightened shepherds, and they looked upward at the angel in glad amazement.

The angel continued, "And this shall be a sign unto you. Ye shall find the babe wrapped in swaddling clothes, lying in a manger."

As the angel finished speaking, the heavens suddenly opened wide. And there, in the brilliant sky, were hundreds of glorious heavenly beings. The air filled with their exquisite voices as they praised God, saying, "Glory to God in the highest, and on earth peace, good will toward men."

The angels continued their heavenly praise, while the shepherds watched and listened with

wondering awe. Then, just as suddenly as it had all begun, the heavens closed again, leaving the hillside dark and quiet. Hushed and silent, the shepherds felt their hearts overflow with reverence and gratitude for the glorious things they had seen and heard.

Matthew thought he might burst with happiness. He had been really happy before—like on his last birthday, when he had gotten just what he wanted—but this was much more than that kind of happiness. This happiness was filled with love— love that reached every part of his body, right down to the ends of his fingertips and toes. And in his heart, Matthew couldn't help wishing that this feeling would never go away.

Chapter Nine

Back to Bethlehem

As the shepherds stood wondering at all that had happened, Nathaniel softly spoke. "The prophets have written that the Savior of the world would be born in the town of Bethlehem," he said, "but I never thought I would be here when it happened. Dear friends, it is a great honor that we are among the first to know that He has come."

Eli was puzzled. "Father, why would the Messiah be laid in a manger, instead of a palace?" he asked.

Nathaniel thought for a moment. "Perhaps it is

to show that He comes for all men, not for just the rich and powerful."

"You mean that He has come to help even humble shepherds like us? Oh, Father," Eli said, "I have never felt the way I feel tonight. Heaven must feel like this."

Nathaniel smiled down at his son and said, "Yes, Eli. I believe that it does."

Then Nathaniel turned to all the shepherds gathered on the hillside. "Now we must follow the angel's instructions. Let us go to Bethlehem and find the baby." With Nathaniel leading the way, the shepherds banded together, making their way to Bethlehem.

Matthew watched them go, and then looked to Katie and said hopefully, "Do you think we could go along?"

"Yes, please! I want to see baby Jesus, too!" pleaded Peter softly.

Katie replied, "Okay, let's follow the shepherds into Bethlehem. We'll have to walk quickly, though. They are hurrying to do as the angel said."

The children hastened to join the group moving

toward the city. As they walked, the shepherds talked quietly among themselves. "Swaddling clothes . . . a manger . . . How will we ever find Him?"

Nathaniel, who was walking at the head of the group, turned to the worried shepherds. "Surely if God sent an angel to tell us the Messiah is born, He will help us find the child." The shepherds, inspired by Nathaniel's faith, nodded in agreement and quickened their steps toward the slumbering little town.

As she traveled down the hillside, Katie looked again toward the heavens where only moments before an angel had appeared. She stopped, at first surprised, and then touched, by what she saw.

"Look," she whispered. "In the place where the angel stood, there is a star."

"It's so bright!" exclaimed Matthew in astonishment. "I've never seen a star glow like that!"

"That's because this star is special," explained Katie. "This star is the sign that Jesus is born. There is no other star like it."

As they followed the shepherds, the children marveled at the sign above them in the heavens. They had read about this star, but never imagined that they, too, would follow it.

With the tranquil surroundings lit by the glorious star overhead, the small band of shepherds traveled quickly along the hillside paths they knew so well. Before long, they entered the silent, peaceful streets of Bethlehem. Katie, Matthew, and Peter were taken by surprise at the change in the town by night. Gone were the bustling people, the noisy animals, and the animated shopkeepers selling their merchandise. The once bustling streets now lay dark and empty and serene.

The children were grateful that some of the shepherds, especially Nathaniel, seemed sure of their way. They traveled through the streets quietly, but with certainty, almost as if they were being guided. Suddenly, Nathaniel stopped. He gathered the shepherds together and turned into a now empty, silent courtyard where an old wooden well stood, lit by the light of the star.

Following behind, the children paused at the entrance to the courtyard and smiled at each other. This place was familiar to them, even in the dark.

Chapter Ten

And They Found the Babe

"Father," said Eli softly. "We are close, aren't we?"

Nathaniel nodded slowly and put his finger to his lips. Here in the courtyard the light from the glorious star seemed especially bright. Here the joyous feelings brought by the angel were even stronger. Surely, this was the place the shepherds sought.

Nathaniel and Eli led the way through the courtyard to the stable's entrance. There, father and son fell to their knees in hushed reverence. The other shepherds followed, and they, too, knelt in worship. Katie, Matthew, and Peter lingered in the shadows and dropped to their knees as they gazed at the scene before them.

It was just as the angel had said it would be. Under the light of star, they had found "the babe wrapped in swaddling clothes, lying in a manger." There was the beautiful baby, wrapped in long, soft pieces of light cloth, resting in a trough full of sweet hay. Mary lay nearby on a bed of clean straw, while Joseph stroked the baby's forehead, humming softly to soothe Him. Then Joseph bowed his head.

Peter whispered, "I think he is saying a prayer."

"Yes," Katie answered, nodding. "Perhaps he is thanking Heavenly Father that Jesus is here safely, and that Mary is all right."

"I think he's thanking Heavenly Father for trusting him to take care of Jesus and Mary," said Matthew, filled with newfound respect for Joseph.

"He could be praying for Heavenly Father's help," added Peter.

"He's probably praying for all those things," Katie said knowingly.

At the end of his prayer, Joseph lifted his head and saw the shepherds kneeling at the door of the stable. Surprised by their presence, but touched by their humble manner, he smiled, and crossed the stable to the doorway where they knelt.

"Sir," Nathaniel began gently, "please forgive us for intruding, but we were sent to find the baby."

"I see," replied Joseph softly. And then, curious, he asked, "Who was it who sent you?"

Nathaniel, not sure how to begin, bowed his head. Slowly, the words formed in his mouth, "We are humble shepherds who were in the fields watching our flocks, when suddenly . . . suddenly . . ." Nathaniel paused again, realizing that what he was about to say might be hard to believe.

"Yes?" encouraged Joseph. "Please, go on."

Taking courage from Joseph's invitation, and filled with certainty about what he had witnessed, Nathaniel continued. "We—all of us—were in the fields tending our flocks, when a glorious light shone down from the heavens. And in the middle of the light was . . . was . . . an angel." Nathaniel looked at the shepherds who nodded in quiet agreement.

As Joseph listened to the testimony of the worshipful shepherds, tears filled his tender eyes.

"Sir, is there something wrong?" Nathaniel asked, afraid he had in some way offended him.

"Oh, no," replied Joseph. "Not at all."

"The angel spoke to us and told us not to be afraid," Nathaniel continued. "He told us the Savior, Christ the Lord, was born and that we would find Him wrapped in swaddling clothes, lying in a manger."

"Is that all?" Joseph asked.

"Oh, no, sir. Then, very suddenly, there were angels filling the whole sky, praising God."

"And proclaiming peace on earth to all men," Eli added eagerly.

Joseph smiled and nodded knowingly. "Yes, my boy. Peace on earth. The prophets foretold that He would be known as the Prince of Peace."

Nathaniel put his hand to his heart. "Ever since the angel appeared, we have felt such a wonderful peace inside."

Joseph nodded. "I have come to know that feeling well." Then, reaching out his hand in friendship, Joseph said, "Please, will you tell me your name?"

"Sir, I am called Nathaniel."

"Nathaniel, like the prophet," Joseph said warmly, as he clasped the shepherd's hand. "Your name means 'gift of God.' It has special meaning tonight, doesn't it? For we are in the presence of God's greatest gift to the world." Joseph looked tenderly at the tiny baby asleep in the hay. "I am Joseph, a carpenter from Nazareth. And you, Nathaniel, are a shepherd from Bethlehem. But we have both been chosen to welcome the Son of God to the earth. Tonight, Nathaniel, you and I are brothers."

Eli stepped forward and asked, "Please, sir. What will you name the baby?"

"His name is Jesus," answered Joseph. "What is your name, son?"

"My name is Eli," the boy replied.

"Well, Eli, just as God sent an angel to you, I was also visited by an angel—long before this child was born. The angel told me of the coming of the child, and he told me that His name would be Jesus. We did not choose His name. God, His Father, did. You see, Eli, this child is not my son. He is the Son of the living God."

Then Joseph stretched out his hand toward the manger. "Come," he beckoned the shepherds, "come and see."

Reverently, the shepherds crept toward the beautiful child. Mary, looking on from her resting place near the manger, smiled her approval. "Come close," she said, beckoning to Eli. "We are grateful that God has not let Him come into the world alone. Thank you for coming to welcome Him."

As the shepherds neared the manger, they bowed their heads in devotion. And Eli, his eyes bright with adoration, leaned forward and gently kissed the baby's forehead. Then he and the others respectfully drew back, their faces radiating the knowledge that they were in the presence of the long-promised Messiah.

Joseph smiled his appreciation. "It is fitting that shepherds would come to welcome Him. The prophet Isaiah wrote that He will feed his flock like a shepherd—just as you feed your flock, Eli," Joseph explained.

"But who is His flock?" asked Eli.

Joseph smiled tenderly and, looking around at all who had come to worship Jesus, answered, "We are, Eli. You, me—all of us. We are His flock, if we choose to follow Him."

The three children from another time looked at each other, their eyes full of promise and determination. And there, at the entrance to the stable, unnoticed by Mary, Joseph, or the shepherds, Katie, Matthew, and Peter silently pledged in their hearts to follow Jesus, the Savior of the world.

Chapter Eleven

The Gift of Love

Then, their hearts overflowing with love, Katie, Matthew, and Peter stepped back into the courtyard. Though not a word was said, somehow they each knew it was time to return to Grandma's cottage. Clasping their hands together, the children suddenly felt themselves lifted away from the stable, away from the courtyard, away from Bethlehem. And in no time at all, Matthew, Katie, and Peter found themselves sitting again on the pillows at Grandma's feet—and Grandma was still reading!

"'But Mary kept all these things and pondered them in her heart,'" she finished and slowly closed the Bible. Grandma was quiet for a moment, and then looked down at her grandchildren. She began softly, "I love reading that story. Jesus came to earth in such a humble, lowly way. And yet, He gave us the greatest gift the world has ever known—the gift of His love."

"Well, then maybe what the shepherds gave to Him was better than I thought," Matthew mused. "All they had to give was *their* love, you know."

"You are a wise boy, Matthew. I've received many gifts in my life," Grandma said. "Like when I married your grandfather. People gave us crystal dishes, fine china, even envelopes full of money— just like the Wise Men who brought gifts of gold, frankincense, and myrrh, I guess."

"What was your favorite present?" Katie asked eagerly.

"Hey! Where *were* the Wise Men?" Peter blurted out before Grandma could answer Katie's question. "I didn't see *them* in the stable!"

Katie quickly corrected him. "I think you mean that you didn't hear Grandma *say* they were in the stable when she was reading."

"Right!" Peter quickly saw his mistake. "That's exactly what I meant."

"Well, Peter," Grandma explained, "the Wise Men were far away from Bethlehem the night Jesus was born. Remember how the scriptures say that they came from the east? It took them a very long time to travel to Palestine to bring their gifts to Jesus—probably a year or two."

"I didn't know that!" exclaimed Peter. "So Jesus had to wait at least a year to get those really expensive presents?"

"Yes, I suppose He did," Grandma agreed. "But no matter how costly those gifts, they couldn't have meant more to Him than the simple love of the shepherds." She smiled as she slipped her arm around her grandson.

"I still want to know about your favorite wedding present, Grandma," Katie reminded her.

"Oh, that's easy," she replied. "I received many

beautiful things. But the gift I treasure the most"—both Matthew and Katie leaned forward to hear what Grandma was going to say—"is a letter from my mother. It tells about the love she felt for me on the day I was born, and how that love became even stronger through the years. Whenever I feel sad or worried, I read that letter. And every time I read it, I feel my mother's love. Love turns sadness to happiness, and worry to peace. Just like for Jesus and the shepherds, love is the best gift I've ever given or received."

Suddenly, Katie knew exactly what to give Grandma this Christmas, and it wouldn't cost a penny. Along with the shepherds at the stable, Katie had been filled with Jesus' love. And now she knew that all she had to do to feel that love again was to share it.

The children settled down to write in their journals as was their tradition on these special visits with Grandma.

"Hey, sis, do you know what you're going to give Grandma yet?" Matthew whispered to Katie.

"I sure do. No doubt about it." Katie smiled as she opened her journal and began a letter:

Dear Grandma,
I can think of a hundred reasons why I love you with all my heart, but the first one is, because you love me.

It worked! As she wrote, the love she felt in the stable was all around her. Grandma must have felt it, too, because as her grandchildren wrote, she smiled as she rocked in her chair and softly sang:

Be near me, Lord Jesus; I ask thee to stay
Close by me forever, and love me, I pray.
Bless all the dear children in thy tender care
And fit us for heaven to live with Thee there.

About the Authors

Alice W. Johnson, a published author and composer, is a featured speaker for youth groups, adult firesides, and women's seminars. A former executive in a worldwide strategy consulting company, and then in a leadership training firm, Alice is now a homemaker living in Eagle, Idaho, with her husband and their four young children.

Allison H. Warner gained her early experience living with her family in countries around the world. Returning to the United States as a young woman, she began her vocation as an actress and writer, developing and performing in such productions as *The Farley Family Reunion*. She and her husband reside in Provo, Utah, where they are raising two active boys.

About the Illustrator

Jerry Harston holds a degree in graphic design and has illustrated more than thirty children's books. He has received many honors for his art, and his clients include numerous Fortune 500 corporations. Jerry and his wife, Libby, live in Sandy, Utah. Their six children and sixteen grandchildren serve as excellent critics for his illustrations.